GARDENS
for the NEW
COUNTRY PLACE

The Landscape Architecture of
Edmund Hollander and Maryanne Connelly

PRINCIPAL PHOTOGRAPHY BY
BETSY PINOVER SCHIFF

ADDITIONAL PHOTOGRAPHY BY
CHARLES MAYER
TORI BUTT
DENCY KANE
STEVE TURNER

GARDENS
for the NEW
COUNTRY PLACE

Contemporary Country Gardens and Inspiring Landscape Elements

BY PAUL BENNETT

Copyright © 2003 by:
EDMUND D. HOLLANDER LANDSCAPE ARCHITECT DESIGN P.C.
153 WAVERLY PLACE, 3RD FLOOR
NEW YORK, NY 10014

Photography:
COPYRIGHT © BETSY PINOVER SCHIFF, ALL RIGHTS RESERVED

Packaged by:
GRAYSON PUBLISHING
JAMES G. TRULOVE, PUBLISHER
1250 28TH STREET NW
WASHINGTON, DC 20007
202-337-1380
JTRULOVE@AOL.COM

Design:
JAMES PITTMAN

First published in 2003
WATSON-GUPTILL PUBLICATIONS, A DIVISION OF
VNU BUSINESS MEDIA INC.,
770 BROADWAY, NEW YORK, NY 10003
WWW.WATSONGUPTILL.COM

LIBRARY OF CONGRESS CONTROL NUMBER: 2003108977

ISBN: 0-8230-2077-0

Manufactured in China
First Printing, 2003

1 2 3 4 5 6 7 8 9 / 06 05 04 03

*This book is dedicated to Ian McHarg, who introduced both
of us to landscape architecture. It was Ian's vision of the earth
as a multilayered living organism deserving the highest level of
reverence and his larger-than-life personality that so inspired
us to take this journey.*

— Edmund Hollander and Maryanne Connelly

*To Wendy and Renata, who have always been there for me
and have tolerated the early mornings, late evenings and
weekend absences when I have been out in the field chasing
my dream of a perfect landscape.*

*And to Jean, whose wisdom and concern only a mother and
ex-television producer could contribute.*

— Edmund Hollander

Contents

Introduction

Great landscapes are like great art: They transport you from the mundane, quotidian drudgery of this world to a place that is ideal and sublime. Examples of such outstanding public landscapes are Central and Prospect Parks in New York, Dumbarton Oaks in Washington, Bloedel Preserve in Seattle, and the Miller Garden in Indiana.

There is, however, a scarcity of great private landscapes. In the last fifty years we've witnessed a gradual degradation in the grandeur and artfulness of private residences where the suburban garden has trumped the American estate, even on estate-sized properties. Instead of sensitive, tasteful designs that express the importance of place, we see garishness, imitation, and a general lack of creativity that hardly approximate the grandeur of the past. Are there new American estates that rival those of yesteryear?

Hidden throughout the New York metropolitan area, a region rich in the history of landscape art, are private estates designed by two New York landscape architects who, for the last ten years, have been developing their own original style. Edmund Hollander and Maryanne Connelly, who have practiced under the name Edmund Hollander Landscape Architect Design P.C., have brought a style that is reminiscent of past grandeur, but can be considered the new American estate. It is, to use the terminology now in vogue in landscape architecture circles, firmly anchored in the context of place — in this case, the history-rich geography of Long Island, Connecticut, and Westchester — much like the great landscape estates of the past.

When you enter a Hollander landscape you are suddenly quite aware of what architects refer to as scale and structure. Most keenly, you perceive a division of the overall property into distinct "rooms," each of which has a purpose and identity and all of which are neatly linked into a necessary sequence. This perfect connection between spaces arises from a deep understanding of land that is both scientific and poetic. With every new client and every new project, Hollander and Connelly spend countless hours studying and analyzing existing conditions — topography, geology, hydrology, and ecology — in order to create a design that not only works physically, so that the first hard rain doesn't wash it all away, but emerges from a place rather than appearing imposed upon it.

The New Country Place

In the context of the New York suburbs, Hollander's work harks back to the so-called Country Place Era at the beginning of the twentieth century, when tycoons with names like Vanderbilt and Phipps built enormous palatial estates outside of the city. The mansions themselves were grand architectural statements, often modeled on European villas and chateaux. The landscape was considered an integral part of the ensemble, and it wasn't uncommon that a patron would spend as much time, energy, and money worrying about the art of the outdoor spaces as he did about the house. This was certainly true of William Vanderbilt's opulent castle in the Great Smoky Mountains, the Biltmore estate, which was built in 1895. Although the mansion is a towering feat of architecture, it is the landscape that is really most notable. Designed by Frederick Law Olmsted, the landscape architect of Central Park, the Biltmore landscape included a mixture of rigidly formal European gardens to complement the house, as well as acres of informal, English-inspired landscape gardens.

On Long Island, as F. Scott Fitzgerald chronicled in *The Great Gatsby*, the Country Place Era was in full swing by the first decade of the new century. Several estates, including Old Westbury, the home of John Phipps, son of an original partner in the Carnegie Steel Corporation, were designed and built lavishly, with acres of gardens surrounding a handsome manor house. Interestingly, "country places" like Old Westbury were intimately familial, despite their grandeur, formality, and large scale. Old Westbury was intended to provide a retreat for Phipps and his extended family away from the increasing bustle of the city. It was a summer home where the family could gather and, for a rare moment, enjoy each other's company before returning to the dynamic atmosphere of New York City.

In design terms it's important to note that, during this era, the natural impulse of the patrons and owners of these estates was to imitate European traditions and surround their homes with extravagant gardens modeled on Italian and French gardens of the past. While landscape architects generally indulged these flights of fancy, they also urged the tycoons to reserve key elements of the design for more regional and contextual designs. For instance, the entry drive was often executed in a more English or American landscape manner, with a romantic, curving roadway that revealed views of the house in a paced, almost rhythmical, manner. Frequently there was a deciduous forest in the design that made connections to the surrounding land. The idea was that at a time when business concerns, and the world in general, seemed to demand so much of the attention of these tycoons and their families, the country place would ground them in an ideal but very real world. In this way, the country place was a distinctly modern idea, reflecting the rapid economic and social changes of America.

The connection between the first decade of the twentieth century and the first of this century is evident. Both are periods of intense economic growth and accumulation of wealth. Accordingly, both are periods characterized by the building of large personal estates — in particular around New York City. Like Mr. Phipps, today's patron is concerned not only with building expansive and expensive homes but also with creating places of art and taste. Likewise, the very best architects and landscape architects who work for them are concerned with appropriateness, drawing from the local, rural, often agricultural, character in order to provide their clients with a place far away from their daily lives. While it would be difficult to follow this characterization too far, one might say we're entering a new Country Place Era in places like Long Island and Greenwich, Connecticut.

Hollander Design's work in the region is a strong indicator of this development. Like the great estates of the past, a Hollander landscape attempts to express regional character and local context. When we view a cross section of the firm's work, there are a few

On Long Island, as F. Scott Fitzgerald chronicled in The Great Gatsby, *the Country Place Era was in full swing by the first decade of the new century.*

apparent facts that bear this out. The most striking is that while the hand of the designer is present in each design, the individual properties express different character. This individual character derives not so much from the difference between clients, but from the difference between contexts — specifically the geographical particularities that make every locale (or region) unique, and each parcel of land separate and distinct from all others. "It all starts with geology," says Edmund Hollander. "On Long Island you have a terminal moraine, which is flat. This natural topography was conducive to agriculture, so the land was cut up into fields and hedgerows; and then later, when the agriculture died, the suburbs that sprouted up there began referring to that agrarian past — large fields, geometric patterning of development, and rural-looking Shingle Style architecture.

"In Greenwich, it's entirely different. The bedrock explodes to the surface. There's a rocky escarpment that runs all the way down to the Long Island Sound, which creates a structure and rhythm in the landscape. That area has always been residential and the houses are fitted — almost organically — in between the rocks and the wetlands." These basic differences — born from tectonic accident and solidified by a couple hundred years of human habitation — give rise to a landscape language that differs from place to place. It is in studying this language that Ed Hollander and Maryanne Connelly begin their work. "Both nature and man make patterns on the land that are visually recognizable," says Hollander. "We start by analyzing this, and then use this basic visual language to create something new."

It is important to understand that this "language" is subtle. Although it surrounds us and absolutely defines the physical world, most of us are absolutely ignorant of the language of landscape. Hollander and Connelly, on the other hand, speak the language fluently. They see a century of estate gardens on Long Island in a simple, old-fashioned hydrangea, or the evolution of an entire landscape in the abrupt twist of bedrock outcropping. In the right hands this subtle grammar can become an extremely potent tool in design. In the hand of Ed Hollander and Maryanne Connelly, this language is translated into a thing of beauty.

A Horticulturist Discovers Design

Edmund Hollander grew up in Manhattan, which is surprising to most of his clients, since his expertise and educational background are in horticulture. But Ed explains that as a kid he spent many weekends on his father's farm in Pennsylvania Dutch Country where the nineteenth-century farm landscapes were dotted with small gardens, overripe with peonies and lilacs. "As a kid I remember burying my face in flowers," recalls Hollander, "and I had this overwhelming sensation that was where my life was going."

At Vassar, Hollander excelled in botany, and after cataloguing the entire tree collection on campus for his senior project, he attended the New York Botanical Garden's professional certification program. "I thought I wanted to be an urban forester," he says. "I was interested in ecology and the larger context of plants." But in Manhattan, where Hollander invariably returned, there weren't many jobs for urban foresters. So he went back to school, this time to the University of Pennsylvania to study landscape architecture.

The University of Pennsylvania landscape architecture program, at the time, was under the influence of two very prominent personalities. The first was Laurie Olin, a landscape architect who would go on to design Bryant Park and Walker Park (part of Battery Park City) in New York, as well as several other important, internationally recognized commissions. The other guiding spirit at Penn at the time was Ian McHarg, whose book *Design with Nature* was revolutionizing the way landscape architects and planners thought about design. McHarg passionately believed that landscape architecture needed to respond to the specific conditions of land. Instead of touting lofty design theories that could be applied across the board to any landscape, McHarg became known for his "layer-cake" system of parsing a landscape into its component parts and then studying them as integrated layers. This had the advantage of focusing the designer upon the peculiarities, uniqueness, and character of individual landscapes. McHarg's layers typically included geology, history, ecology, and anything else that might contribute to creating a sense of place. Each place is different; therefore design has to evolve and change from place to place. A keen thinker and persuasive rhetorician, McHarg argued that it might even be immoral for landscape architects to disregard the "layers" that give a place its identity. At a time when blanket design theories were very much in vogue, it was a radical proposition.

Hollander took an introductory class with McHarg called "Design of the Environment," which brought together architecture students, planning students, and landscape students in one place and presented them with this holistic, broad vision of the world. Ed was knocked off his feet. "I remember suddenly learning that landscape architecture would never be a singular thing. It would always be part of something larger, such as a part of architecture, a part of a town or city, and a part of nature." Hollander took a job with McHarg in order to work his way through school and ended up out on a farm in West Chester, Pennsylvania — located just on the cusp of the Dutch Country he'd known as a youth — where he helped his mentor develop his private property. He also did some work in McHarg's studio, helping to design a headquarters for the Girl Scouts. And although he continued to study plants and horticulture, his interests were becoming distinctly "McHargian." As Hollander was coming into his own he looked for connections and context. He began to see the land as a series of interrelated parts in the context of cultural and natural history.

Hollander and Connelly met at the University of Pennsylvania. Connelly's background was in art and biology, and she had originally come to the University of Pennsylvania's Veterinary School to work in ophthalmology research. Her background extended to the Academy of Natural Sciences, where she taught natural science to inner-city high school students. She saw an opportunity to use her experience in science when, like Hollander, she read the McHarg book, *Design with Nature*. She later visited McHarg's design office in Center City, Philadelphia, where she saw regional planners overlaying natural factor maps to design ski trails in Aspen. She was inspired by the possibility of combining science with design. After a year in the Regional Planning Master's Program at the University of Pennsylvania, Connelly transferred to the Landscape Architecture Program, where she met Hollander. A partnership was born, and the two worked together on a variety of projects.

Hollander's emphasis was on plants and horticulture, while Connelly had a natural inclination for design and graphics. Their distinctly different backgrounds have proven to be an asset, with each bringing the kind of perspective that oftentimes, while producing heated discussions, results in a synergy that inspires powerful landscape design.

The Work

The projects that follow are representative of the broad range of the firm's work. Each property, each client, and therefore each landscape is different from the other. Yet, through each runs a set of principles that guide the hand of both Connelly and Hollander, and make the work of Hollander Design read as a whole.

The first principle is the ambition to create *spatial quality* in the landscape. This is a very architectural idea. But Hollander and Connelly are landscape architects, and for them, before any plants go into the ground or any backhoes arrive on the site, questions must be answered. These concern the siting of the house, its architectural composition, and the language of the existing landscape, both in terms of the local and regional context and the actual site conditions on the property. Physically, spatial quality is a matter of scale. For instance, at a residence in Greenwich the house is large, with an extensive patio and verandah located to the southeast, but at the rear of the property. The spatial quality of the landscape therefore needed to be equally impressive. A delicate garden would have been lost in the space, and a tennis court or other recreational facility would have disturbed the majestic rhythm of the handsome façade. Instead, Hollander and Connelly crafted a sweeping lawn that drifts away from the house in a large expanse toward the woods in the distance. It creates an open quality in response to the open quality of the house itself.

Creating a dialogue between architecture and landscape is the second principle at work in these projects. "We try to work side by side with the architects from day one," says Hollander, "collaborating on the siting of the house, and then taking cues from their designs to inform our own." Hollander and Connelly respect and admire the collaborative efforts of garden designer Gertrude Jekyll and the architect Edwin Lutyens, who were hailed on both sides of the Altlantic for their Cottage-Style residences in early twentieth century England. For Hollander, the great success of Jekyll and Lutyens was to be found in the continuity and seamlessness of their work. "There was a synthesis and integration between the landscape and architecture," Hollander pointed out. "They worked together, not as imitations of one another, but as two voices in a dialogue. This is the kind of thing we strive for." In their work, Hollander and Connelly look for moments in the architecture where ideas or themes can be extended and repeated in the landscape. Perhaps it is a bit of stonework that can be used as a retaining wall. Or perhaps it is the rhythm of a cornice that is expanded upon in the massing of a hedge. Sometimes it is a subtle, sometimes an obvious, dialogue.

The last principle that guides the work is a concern with the *transitional moments* in the landscape. These are the spaces, usually close to the house, where the eye or the body moves from one well-defined space into another. For Connelly these are the most important places in the landscape. "It's when you step from inside to outside, or from a sunny spot to a shady spot, or from a formal area to an informal," said Connelly. "We try to emphasize those transitions so that you have an experience of moving through the landscape as a whole, logical sequence." The analogy to music is obvious. Hollander and Connelly like to see the landscape as a series of spaces or movements linked together by transitions or segues that set a tone for the perceiver. In the projects that follow, without exception, there are key transition spaces. It might be where the living space of the house opens onto a terrace, or where a terrace segues into a planted area, or where a garden path turns a corner into an open expanse of lawn. These are spaces that Hollander and Connelly cherish, where the landscape experience reaches a threshold before giving way to something new.

With these three principles lying like roots in soil to feed every new design, Hollander and Connelly have developed, over the last ten years, a method of working. First, they consider the site and, in McHargian fashion, the ecological and contextual factors that affect it. Secondly, they consider the architectural style of the house. Having worked with a range of architects from Steven Holl to Robert A. M. Stern, the firm has become familiar with diverse styles — all along looking for the ways in which specific architecture impacts landscape. And lastly, they look to the client and the individual needs that must be addressed in a landscape that, like the country places of yesterday, needs to be both formal and familial. So, here we see magic tricks of sorts: play areas for children integrated with rose gardens for mom, a putting green for dad together with a strolling woods for elderly parents. The technical term for these seemingly competing needs is "program," and in the milieu of private residences a designer's mettle is very much determined by his ability to juggle programs without sacrificing art. How do you include a tennis court and cutting garden on a three-acre site without destroying the million-dollar view? These are the challenges that keep landscape architecture exciting for Connelly and Hollander.

The analogy to music is obvious. Hollander and Connelly like to see the landscape as a series of spaces or movements linked together by transitions or segues that set a tone for the perceiver.

Rooster Hill

The rolling hills north of New York City have been horse country for nearly three hundred years. As a result, the landscape itself is inscribed with the language of barns, paddocks, open vistas of mist-covered hills with the line of a wooden pasture fence in the foreground, and other vernacular remainders of its agrarian past.

It was this agrarian past that Hollander Design used as its inspiration for a twenty-acre estate set on a knoll in North Salem. THE MAIN HOUSE IS SET UPON THE HILL TO TAKE ADVANTAGE OF THE VIEWS OF THE SURROUNDING HILLS AND A LAKE IN THE DISTANCE. DESCENDING DOWN A STEEP SLOPE, THE LIVING LAND-SCAPE OF TERRACES EVOLVES INTO A POOL PATIO. The remaining land is derived from the language of farming. The entrance drive arcs gently through an allée of sugar maples (*Acer saccharum*) and Red Sunset maples (*Acer rubrum* 'Red Sunset'). The drive curves a path between two black paddock fences that enclose a dressage ring on one side and a pasture for Belted Galloway cattle on the other.

Classic stone walls enclose the entry court, which works as a sort of viewing platform for the surrounding landscape. Here, connelly and hollander used stone as an element of visual linkage, connecting the house to the entry court and the court to the barn. The design of the barn (massive stone base, gabled roof, dormer windows, etc.) was derived from a study of barn architecture in the surrounding area.

ABOVE: *The pool terrace extends past the end of the pool, offering dramatic views to the lake beyond.*

FAR LEFT: *Seating is arranged to look over the pool with its negative edge.*

LEFT: *The negative edge wall is capped with bluestone, and the fieldstone facing gives the impression of a waterfall from below.*

RIGHT: *Infinity edge pool, spa, and terrace create a setting for the pool house by Mojo Stumer Architects.*

During the site planning for the property, it became obvious that one of the key features of the design was the stunning view. In order to preserve this, the pool was set away from the house and tucked into the side of the hill so that it remains hidden from the dining and living terraces adjoining the house. It is accessed by a series of lawn terraces, held in place by large stone retaining walls, curved to exemplify the natural topography and planted as gardens with flowering shrubs and perennials that bloom from April to October. Spring begins with baptisia, peonies, and irises, which progress into such classic summer flowers as lavender, catmint, phlox, Russian sage, loosestrife, and hollyhock. In the fall, asters, sedum, and Japanese anemone continue the sequence. New Dawn roses grow from and tumble over the walls; Annabelle and Nikko hydrangeas provide masses of blue and white color through the summer, while Pee Gee hydrangea trees mark the landings at the top of each staircase. THE POOL ITSELF WAS DESIGNED WITH A NEGATIVE EDGE TO MAKE A VISUAL CONNECTION WITH THE LAKE BEYOND AND, ON DAYS OF BRILLIANT SUN, TO CREATE THE VISUAL ILLUSION FROM CERTAIN ANGLES THAT THEY ARE ONE AND THE SAME. Even further below this lies a newly-planted orchard of heirloom apples.

Ever watchful for existing elements that can be highlighted, Hollander and Connelly had a rock outcrop exposed that counterbalances the composition of spaces and forms. Unique microclimates found in the crevices allowed for a garden of mosses and alpine plants.

The overall design strives for cleanliness and simplicity — a refined and measured aesthetic that anchors the landscape in the context of its agrarian surroundings.

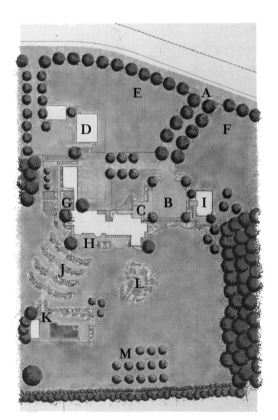

A Maple-Lined Entry Drive
B Cherry Blossom Court
C Entry Terrace
D Barn
E Paddock
F Riding Ring
G Vegetable/Herb Garden
H Rear Terrace
I Guest House
J Walled Garden
K Pool Area
L Outcrop Garden
M Orchard

TOP: *Paddock fencing lines the entry drive.*

ABOVE: *The entry terrace flows out from the front door to the parking court as a result of the collaboration of architect and land-scape architect.*

RIGHT: *Stone walls define spaces in both the horizontal and vertical plans.*

ABOVE: *Belted Galloway cattle graze in front of the barn.*

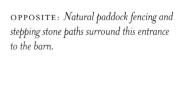

OPPOSITE: *Natural paddock fencing and stepping stone paths surround this entrance to the barn.*

ABOVE: *Steps to the barn and paddock.*

RIGHT: *Walls by Mike Cobuzzi separate and connect the barn area with the house.*

LEFT: *Dry-stacked stone walls create a backdrop for gardens planted with Pee Gee hydrangea trees, New Dawn roses, phlox, iris, lavender and other summer-blooming perennials.*

ABOVE: *Curved bluestone stairs lead up from the pool to the rear of the house.*

FOLLOWING PAGES LEFT: *The orchard is separated from the lower fields by a rebuilt country stone wall.*

FOLLOWING PAGES RIGHT: *View across the orchard to the lake and rolling hills beyond.*

Pond View

The landscape in this locale is much more lush and dense than the more oceanic areas nearby. Here we find mature stands of woodland. The residential plots are demarcated by hedges and lines of blooming plants that create a sense of depth and color in shaded areas. The houses are fitted in among the trees, rather than standing alone on the plain.

For this residence, the challenge confronting Connelly and Hollander was how to work with the existing tree cover to create an experience of alternating light and shade. The house is approached by a subtly arcing drive, lined with granite and overplanted with a light deciduous canopy. The expanse of lawn and spacing of single trees recall the old Olmsted-designed estates of the early twentieth century. Immediately adjacent to the house and serving as a transition space between the interior living area and the pool terrace lies a shade garden. Hostas, astilbes, bluebells, and whitewashed architectural arbors and arches covered in creeping vines combine to create a cool oasis. Existing mature trees are used as visual focal points for the paths as they work in a grid from house to terrace. At points the canopy opens briefly, and here we find rivers of color — pink climbing roses and Pee Gee hydrangeas underpinned by pink peonies and accented by such architectural details as a simple wooden fence.

HOLLANDER AND CONNELLY ORGANIZED THE LANDSCAPE SO THAT ONE PROCEEDS, EITHER PHYSICALLY OR VISUALLY, IN A LINEAR FASHION FROM THE HOUSE TO THE WETLAND. Two hyperbolic walking paths lined with old-fashioned roses, hollyhocks, purple loosestrife, and lavender radiate out from the pool terrace, enclosing a grass lawn. In the center of the view lies a small boathouse, around which is planted a willow grove that refracts the light and makes a quiet destination in the landscape. Along the far edge of the property, where it gives over to a wetland and pond, Hollander created a transitional garden with wet-rooted flowering plants that attract a variety of butterflies.

TOP: *Wooden gates with stone columns mark the entry to the property.*

MIDDLE: *A broad gravel drive cuts through the lawn leading up to the entry court.*

BOTTOM: *A bluestone terrace bordered by blue lace hydrangea and pink fairy roses greets visitors at the front door.*

RIGHT: *The gate from the pool area leads to a shaded gravel walk amongst beds of astilbe and hosta under a venerable old maple tree.*

"A lot of work was done here rearranging things," Connelly notes. "There were hedges and lines dissecting the property, and a general confusion to the layout." One of the key clarifying gestures was locating the pool to the side of the main view and axis so that the primary relationship between the house and water was maintained and uninterrupted.

The landscape is treated as an ensemble; individual rooms are knitted together in a linear structure that is described by the relationship between the house and the pond. Everything moves in parallel from one to the other. The controlling mechanism consists of lines of hedge and pathways, which create visual depth in the naturally dense landscape.

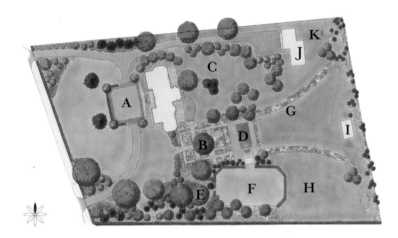

A *Entry Court*
B *Shade Garden*
C *Cryptomeria Garden*
D *Pool Area*
E *Woodland Walk*
F *Tennis Court*
G *Garden Path Borders Leading to Pond*
H *Cutting Garden*
I *Boathouse*
J *Guest House*
K *Guest House Garden*

LEFT: *A wooden picket fence detailed to match the porches on the house is covered in Eden and Constance Spry roses.*

BELOW LEFT: *Constance Spry roses cover the picket fence surrounding the spa terrace.*

RIGHT: *The pool area overlooks the garden paths leading down to the pond.*

LEFT: *Looking across the new lawn and garden borders to an arbor that marks the entry to the cutting garden.*

TOP: *The path is bordered by Russian sage, hollyhocks, loosestrife, and catmint.*

ABOVE: *Bluestone and fieldstone stairs lead up to one of the pool area gates.*

LEFT: *The arbor and gate leading into the cutting garden is covered in the blooms of fragrant Sweet Autumn clematis.*

TOP: *Looking toward the house from the boathouse porch.*

ABOVE: *Working with architect Francis Fleetwood, the house was sited to preserve an ancient grove of cryptomeria trees.*

ABOVE: *Gardens lining the walk to the pond partially obscure the way into the cutting garden.*

FOLLOWING PAGES: *The cutting garden has Pee Gee hydrangea trees as its focal point.*

Windswept

Creating a dialogue between landscape and architecture is one of the hallmarks of Hollander Design. For this ten-acre residence, set in the meadows along the edge of an ocean-side pond, Hollander and Connelly took their cues both from the house and the surrounding land. The dual forms of the rectangle and the semicircle are prevalent in the design of the house, the meadow plots, and undulating shoreline of the pond. The landscape, in turn, echoes these shapes in key places, creating a kind of fitness of design that makes everything work together. Close to the house lay a pool terrace and herb garden, both rectangular and fitted into the architecture. Linking them is a semicircular stone terrace traced with creeping thyme, which makes a visual connection to the grand central porch nearby that looks out over a vista of the pond. THE LAWN, CUT IN A SQUARE FROM THE COUNTRYSIDE, AGAIN REFERS TO THE RECTANGULAR BASE OF THE ARCHITECTURE, WHILE A SIMPLE CURVE OF HYDRANGEAS SET A SLIGHT DISTANCE FROM THE PORCH REVIVES THE SEMICIRCULAR FORM.

Close in upon the house, the gardens serve as outdoor rooms. The stepped culinary gardens are filled with varieties of herbs and complementary plantings such as perovskia, nepeta, and various salvias. The visual effect is of a sea of gray-green topped with flowing blue and purple flowers. The pool terrace is the most formal space, with capped post fence and effusion of blooming plants, including old fashioned Eden climbing roses, white phlox, Casa Blanca lilies,

pink and purple loosestrife, mallow, lavender, and coreopsis. The terrace is raised above the level of the yard in order to open a vista toward the pond and the ocean beyond. However, the aesthetic is rooted in the agricultural, summer-residence feel of the area, which is evoked by the strong use of brick, fieldstone, and sun-bleached wood. The plants are salt-tolerant and left to grow in a wild, Cottage-Style manner reminiscent of Gertrude Jekyll and William Robinson.

LEFT: *The outdoor shower provides a view over the gardens and pool area to the pond in the distance.*

RIGHT: *The pool area is set 18 inches above grade, requiring only a 30-inch fence from the inside. This helps to tie the area to the lawn, meadow, and pond.*

Set off a distance from the house is a sunken tennis court surrounded by a "wave garden." This is composed of undulating mounds sculpted to resemble waves when viewed from eye level. The mounds are planted with a variety of white flowering shrubs that look like white foam on the crests of breaking waves. These include: *Spirea nipponica* 'Snowmound,' Annabelle hydrangea, shrubby cinquefoil (*Potentilla fruticosa* 'Abbotswood'), viburnum, and several varieties of *Hydrangea paniculata*, including the early-blooming 'Kyushu,' mid-season 'Unique,' and late-blooming 'Tardiva.' Because the surrounding topography contains gentle grade shifts, from flat meadow to shoreline to slight wooded rises, Hollander molded the tennis court gently into the landscape so that the entry path — a romantic gesture of sloping grass with bluestone risers, enclosed by white hydrangeas and river birch trees — creates a graceful transition from the house to the court.

In order to fit the house into its local context, a good deal of native meadow was stitched into the design in key places. The long entry drive, a rhythmic curving path, winds through a grove of salt-tolerant locusts that are matched to the clay soils. The drive is bordered with lawn that transitions to pasture meadow planted with andropogon, panicum, and other native fescue grasses. The species were specifically chosen to lie low and grow to a uniform height so that ocean breezes would flow through the grasses to create a visual effect and remind the observer that he or she was at the threshold of the sea. At the entrance, the presentation culminates — or rather begins — in an apple orchard that was rescued from a nearby field just before the trees were bulldozed. As a reminder of the vernacular agricultural landscape, the orchard sets up a kind of theatrical presentation upon entry: As we proceed from the farmland through the garden to the edge of the sea, the landscape communicates a subtle shift — plants evolve, light changes, the space is reinvented.

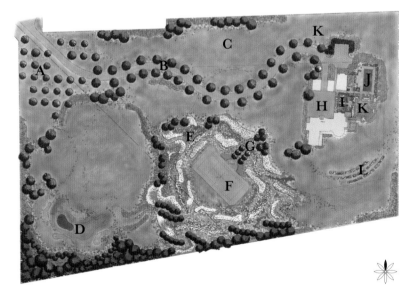

A *Entry Orchard*
B *Locust-Lined Drive*
C *Meadow Areas*
D *Golf Green*
E *"Wave Garden"*
F *Sunken Tennis Court*
G *Birch Walk to Tennis Court*
H *Entry Court*
I *Stepped Kitchen Garden*
J *Pool Area*
K *Living Terrace*
L *Circular Hydrangea Beds*

LEFT: *A curved wall of Pennsylvania fieldstone embraces the main living terrace.*

BELOW: *The fieldstone terrace with creeping thyme joints leads up to the gates that allow entry into the pool area.*

RIGHT: *A terrace of random rectangular bluestone surrounds the pool whose color was carefully selected to match the pond and ocean beyond.*

FAR RIGHT: *The stepped kitchen gardens are "watched over" by the outdoor shower.*

BELOW: *An unstained cedar picket fence encloses the pool area and provides support for Eden roses, indigo spires sage, and Morden's pink loosestrife.*

LEFT: *The pergola separates the kitchen garden from the entry court.*

BELOW: *The kitchen garden is set amongst a series of terraced brick walls and paths leading from the pergola down to the living terrace.*

OPPOSITE: *The kitchen garden connects the screened porch and outdoor shower while providing access and views to the living terrace and landscape beyond.*

ABOVE: *Fescue and other meadow grasses transition into the front edge of the "Wave Garden" screening the tennis court.*

BELOW: *View from amongst the "Waves" looking back at the house.*

ABOVE: *Slabs of reclaimed stone with turf treads lead down to the tennis court.*

ABOVE RIGHT: *White lacecap hydrangea and river birch line the walk to the tennis court.*

RIGHT: *A viewing terrace is set amongst ornamental meadow grasses which sway in the near-constant breezes.*

LEFT: *A series of curved beds of hydrangea play off the curved tower of the house and the stone wall emerging from the ground plane in the distance.*

RIGHT: *View from the curved hydrangea beds towards the living terrace.*

MIDDLE RIGHT: *View from across the curved hydrangea beds to the meadow and windswept maple trees.*

BOTTOM RIGHT: *Grass paths allow strolling amongst the hydrangea varieties.*

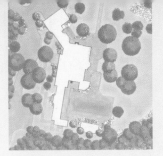

Stepping Walls

This residence was originally designed by Robert A. M. Stern and renovated years later by Bruce Nagel, a protégé of the architect Charles Gwathmey. A recent addition was designed by Leroy Street Architects. The architecture, being both traditional and slightly modern, influenced the landscape, which unfolds in nautilus fashion counterclockwise, starting close to the house on the northern side and opening up moving west and south. WORKING ON A TRANSVERSE AXIS ESTABLISHED BY THE NEW POOL HOUSE AND ADDITION, HOLLANDER DESIGNED A TERRACE OF BLUESTONE AND FIELD-STONE DRY-SET WALLS THAT ECHO THE PALETTE EMPLOYED BY STERN/NAGEL IN THE ORIGINAL HOUSE. A dark pool, fringed by blue hydrangeas, draws the architectural lines out into the landscape. It is a strongly built space that acts, architecturally, almost like a courtyard. The simplicity of the form is echoed in the large open lawn nearby that is structured by a carefully edited woods of mature native oaks. In consultation with Hollander, the client has experimented with making this a transitional area by adding a grove of magnolias (*Magnolia virginiana*) with delightfully fragrant summer-blooming flowers. The gnarled, clumped branching pattern of the magnolias provides a nice contrast to the oaks overhead. This is artfully underplanted with drifts of cinnamon and interrupted fern to create a screen through which another lawn beyond is glimpsed, and then beyond that a white garden. This garden is composed of Mt. Hood and Thalia narcissus, white foxglove, astilbes, bleeding heart, daylilies, and salvia, backed up with Lanarth white and Annabelle hydrangea. Seen through

LEFT: *A wildflower meadow surrounds a stately old pear tree.*

RIGHT: *Walls, stepping-stone path, and garden lead down from the house to the tennis court.*

the thin screen of trees in the foreground, the emphasis is on space, perspective, and light. Landscape architecture, Hollander believes, is in one sense an exercise in manipulating light. Here this idea is expressed through the contrast between the large shady area close to the house and the open sunny lawn beyond.

From a second terrace on the southern face of the house, a path of bluestone squares — Mondrian-like in their precise geometry — descend through a modernist cutting garden. The garden is cut into the slope as four dry-set Pennsylvania fieldstone walls staggered across the lawn. DECORATIVE GRASSES AND PERENNIALS ARE PLANTED IN CLUMPS THAT ACCENTUATE THE GEOMETRY AND EVOLVE FROM A MORE CONTROLLED, "GARDENESQUE" COMPOSITION CLOSER TO THE HOUSE TO A "WILD" AND NATURAL DISPLAY CLOSER TO THE WETLAND. The palette evolves from catmint, Russian sage, black-eyed Susans, and salvia to large grasses like calamagrostis and miscanthus. From the house the gardens are nearly hidden from view, and instead the landscape looks like it sweeps down as a single gesture of lawn to the boggy wildflower meadow beyond. But from within the gardens, the view back to the house unfolds as an effusion of color and variety, a trick of the eye that heightens the experiential character of the landscape.

One of the themes of the design, as it evolved over many years in collaboration with the client and the various architects, was to make connections in the landscape between different areas (house and garden, entry drive and tennis court, etc.) One of the key connections is made visually between the main space of the landscape — the great lawn adjacent to the house — and the surrounding semi-agrarian context. At the bottom of the cascading, modernist garden the landscape evolves into a bog and wildflower meadow that visually opens into a larger empty pasture beyond. The pasture is actually a different property. However, by leaving the edge of the garden open and framed by trees (which has the effect of drawing the eye outward), Hollander creates the illusion that it is all interconnected, that the lawn from this property transitions seamlessly from garden to meadow to pasture, as nature intended.

It is the interplay of overtly artful designs, the gardens, against what looks to be natural providence, the open lawn punctuated by shade trees, that gives the property its character. As a striking example of how this works, the tennis house was originally sited in a way that would have necessitated the removal of a large tupelo tree. Recognizing that this tree would not only give shade to the house and reduce energy costs but that it would create a kind of dialogue between natural context and manmade intrusion, the decision was made to re-site the tennis court. The tree then became a destination at the end of the modernist garden walk, one that serves to symbolize the contrast between nature and art.

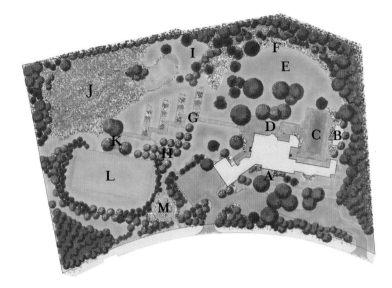

A	Entry Court	H	Orchard
B	Pool House	I	Golf Green
C	Pool Area	J	Perennial Wildflower Meadow
D	Magnolia and Fern Grove	K	Tennis House
E	Wedding Lawn	L	Tennis Court
F	White Border	M	Rose Garden
G	Stepped Garden Walls		

ABOVE RIGHT: *The dark bottom of the pool reflects a specimen dwarf white pine.*

ABOVE LEFT: *Summer-blooming hydrangea help make the transition from pool to yard.*

LEFT: *Looking out through the English border garden to the lawn, walled garden, and wildflower meadow in the distance.*

OPPOSITE: *A 60- by 20-foot pool is set into a bluestone terrace and framed by an English border garden backed up by a fieldstone wall.*

TOP LEFT: *The wedding lawn is bordered by a white garden of Lanarth white hydrangea, nicotiana, and foxglove.*

TOP RIGHT: *A seating area is protected by a grove of sweet bay magnolia set in a glade of cinnamon fern.*

ABOVE LEFT: *View across the walled garden to the rear lawn and the informal white garden in the distance.*

ABOVE RIGHT: *The white border is separated from the lawn by a fieldstone walk.*

OPPOSITE: *The lawn is shaded by native oaks.*

OPPOSITE: *Leading out from the house a triple row of 18-inch-square bluestone pavers looks out over a series of borders that step down and over, leading one out to the tennis house and meadow beyond.*

ABOVE: *Looking back towards the house, one sees the rhythm of the stone walls that create the framework for the stepped gardens.*

ABOVE: *The golf green is surrounded by wildflower meadow and the walled gardens; the tennis house is in the distance.*

LEFT: *Summer wildflowers include Queen Anne's lace, bachelor's buttons, black-eyed Susans, yarrows, and chicory.*

OPPOSITE: *The wildflowers make this approach to the green a challenging shot.*

BELOW: *The tennis house is tucked under an old tupelo tree, which provides shade in the summer months.*

RIGHT: *Nikko blue hydrangea flank the arched opening in the tennis house.*

MIDDLE RIGHT: *The tennis court fencing is planted with honeysuckle and Sweet Autumn clematis.*

BOTTOM RIGHT: *The wisteria pergola provides a shaded venue to watch the tennis.*

LEFT: *Stepping stone–paths lead to the tennis court or the golf green.*

BELOW: *Rhythmically geometric paths lead to the rose garden and backyard.*

OVERLEAF LEFT: *The entry to the rose garden is framed by an arbor with broad fieldstone steps leading up to the rose beds.*

OVERLEAF RIGHT: *A circular path leads around the garden beds with a cut bluestone medallion in the center.*

Old Orchard

This elegant, three-acre village house strikes a soft note in the quickly developing south fork of Long Island. Working with an existing orchard, Hollander enlarged the living space around the house by visually including acreage from an adjacent cottage. As designed by Francis Fleetwood the house features a wraparound hardwood porch open to the landscape. Hollander created a perennial border edge that frames this space, establishing a sense of intimacy and heightening the connection with the surrounding yard. The manipulation is simple. At first glance it seems like nothing more than a porch overlooking a flower garden. But then we realize that there are hundreds of different ways of looking at the flower garden, and that the spatial arrangements — and hence the ways of experiencing the garden — are myriad.

The house is engulfed in boxwood and white Annabelle hydrangea, a simple white/green combination that refers to traditional Hampton summer gardens. Peonies were added to create a symphony of color in June. At the one end of the property lies the remnant of an old apple orchard, which Hollander underplanted with native meadow grasses and wildflowers. The view lines between the porch and the orchard were clarified — the simple, horizontal plane of green lawn serves as a kind of framing device — which has the effect of focusing attention on the crooked, almost sculptural character of the ancient trees.

THE PORCH IS THE FULCRUM OF THE HOUSE — THE POINT AROUND WHICH EVERYTHING ELSE REVOLVES, AND TO WHICH EVERYTHING REFERS. IT NOT ONLY HELPS, AS HOLLANDER PUTS IT, "TO BLUR THE DISTINCTION BETWEEN THE INSIDE AND THE OUTSIDE," BUT IT CREATES A VERY STRUCTURED WAY OF VIEWING THE GARDENS. It is a "peekaboo" design, with certain areas coming into view and then receding as one walks around the small porch. The garden landscape, in turn, is derived from

TOP: *The screened porch is surrounded by a garden of hydrangeas, peonies, and roses.*

ABOVE: *The entry walk is framed with Annabelle hydrangeas and boxwood.*

OPPOSITE: *View across the pool gardens towards the rear of the house.*

the old Cottage-Style gardens of Gertrude Jekyll. Composed in drifts of perennials, it provides an aesthetic interpretation of an idealized country garden, intended to evoke the idea of gentler times and calmer days. This one in particular was designed as a fragrant garden with boxwood hedge, old fashioned roses, and perennials. The client wanted something simple and old-seeming. "You can imagine what it's like to sit out here at six in the evening on a summer day with a gin and tonic," says Hollander.

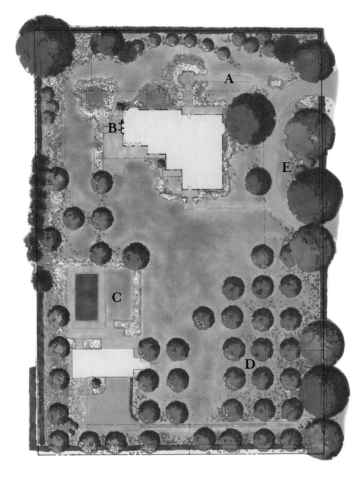

A *Entry Walk*
B *Porch Gardens*
C *Pool Area*
D *Orchard/Wildflower Meadow*
E *Linden Tree Swing*

OPPOSITE: *Looking across the pool, the rose arbor frames a gateway that leads back to the house.*

RIGHT: *An orchard of elegant, old apple trees comes to life in the spring with daffodils, followed by a summer-blooming wildflower meadow.*

BELOW LEFT: *The garden frames a walkway.*

BELOW RIGHT: *A simple stepping-stone path leads to the back door.*

Garden Rooms

This residence is composed as a series of intimate garden rooms connected by swaths of open lawn. The effect is to create a system of alternating spaces, one enclosed and quiet, the other open and sunny. A rhythmic sense evolves as one walks around the house, which creates the focal point for the entire composition.

The granite-lined entrance drive arrives in a square court that, pinned at each corner by mature flowering cherry trees, creates a subdued but elegant setting for the stately manor house. TO ONE SIDE WE GET A GLIMPSE OF THE INTERIOR GARDENS HIDDEN BEHIND A WOODEN FENCE. WE SEE HYDRANGEAS AND WHITE ROSES, BUT FROM THE OUTSIDE, THE MAIN IDEA COMMUNICATED IS ONE OF SECLUSION AND PRIVACY. INSIDE, HOLLANDER WAS ULTIMATELY CONCERNED WITH THE SCALE AND SHAPE OF THE GARDEN SPACES AND HOW THEY RELATE TO THE HOUSE. The most highly evolved garden is really a series of spaces that lies on the southeasterly side of the house. Here we find a "hydrangea walk" that lies on axis with a bay window and serves to extend, visually, the interior space of the house with an exterior vista.

The walk is designed as two rows of mounded white-blooming hydrangeas outlining a grass path. The path culminates in a whitewashed, large-scale pergola that opens the landscape up to a more formal presentation and then transitions into a lavender knot garden, carved in interlocking diamonds and lined with low-clipped boxwood. The entire series reads as a progressively opening space, evolving from the understated and informal hydrangea walk to the highly organized and formal knot garden.

ABOVE: *The formal entry court is punctuated by a cobblestone border and medallion.*

LEFT: *A bust peeks out from the arborvitae hedge into the knot garden.*

RIGHT: *The knot garden has beds of lavender varieties within low boxwood hedges.*

The living space of the house is extended to the rear with a large, rectangular pool terrace. This space is kept open and lined on one side by a large expanse of lawn and on the other with a sun-filled rose garden. The house and pool house form balanced bookends to the landscape and create powerful cross-vistas through the space that is gained from the center of the rose garden looking across the terrace and out into the lawn. Hollander emphasizes the openness of the space by careful placement of architectural elements, most evident in the trellises in the rose garden: latticed steeple structures that frame the view and help to stabilize the open scale of the space.

ON THE FACE OF IT, THE LANDSCAPE SEEMS FORMAL — A ROSE GARDEN CLEAVED INTO QUADRANTS, AN EIGHTEENTH-CENTURY KNOT GARDEN, LAWN VISTAS. IN ORDER TO MAKE THE LANDSCAPE FIT WITH THE LOCAL CONTEXT AND TO TONE DOWN THESE ELEMENTS, HOLLANDER DESIGN CHOSE TO WORK WITH A VERY SIMPLE, RUSTIC PALETTE. The blooms are mostly whites and pinks, and are created by a limited spectrum of roses and hydrangeas set against stately architectural backdrops of fences, pergolas, etc. A certain balance is achieved so that the landscape becomes a place of beauty and proportion.

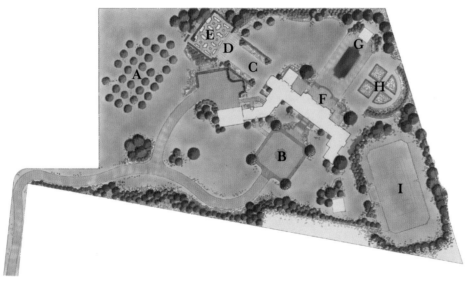

A	*Orchard in Wildflower Meadow*	**F**	*Living Terrace*
B	*Entry Court*	**G**	*Pool Area*
C	*Hydrangea Garden*	**H**	*Rose Garden*
D	*Pergola*	**I**	*Sunken Tennis Court*
E	*Knot Garden*		

ABOVE: *The knot garden.*

OPPOSITE FAR LEFT: *View from the pergola to the hydrangea garden is centered on the family room window of the house.*

OPPOSITE FAR RIGHT: *View from the pergola into the knot garden.*

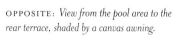

OPPOSITE: *View from the pool area to the rear terrace, shaded by a canvas awning.*

ABOVE: *View of the pool area and rose garden.*

RIGHT: *The pool house completes the axial relationship at the end of the pool terrace.*

OPPOSITE: *The rose garden has grass paths and boxwood-lined beds surrounded by a semicircular evergreen hedge.*

RIGHT: *Lattice obelisks provide vertical elements and support for climbing roses in the garden.*

BELOW RIGHT: *View from the rose garden towards the pool area.*

The Farm

This property refers back to the great Country Place estates of the early twentieth century on every level: scale, design, aesthetics, and functionality. Comprising sixty acres of former dairy farm, the landscape evolves as a series of unfolding experiences, beginning with the entry drive and culminating in the garden rooms surrounding the manor house.

Visitors enter the property by an unassuming country road, purposefully designed to fit within the old farming context of the neighborhood. Several existing barns used by the previous owner for storing feed were saved and restored. They serve as the groundskeeper's office and storehouse, but also work to anchor the landscape in an agrarian aesthetic. THE DRIVE MEANDERS AROUND THE EDGE OF THE PROPERTY, PASSING A NINE-HOLE GOLF COURSE CREATED BY LEGENDARY COURSE DESIGNER REES JONES. THE RHYTHM HERE IS CALCULATED TO DIRECT VIEWS INWARD OVER THE OPEN EXPANSE OF THE COURSE TOWARDS A SERIES OF THREE PONDS. "When we arrived on the scene these ponds were in a serious state of degradation," remembers Hollander. "The farmer had used them as garbage pits. When the dairy industry converted from glass bottles to cardboard cartons he dumped all his old glass bottles here. I think we removed thousands of cubic yards of debris — old bottles, tires, rusted farm tools. You name it." The pond surrounds were developed as wildflower meadows, which blend into the fescue roughs of the golf course to create the illusion that these ponds and the surrounding landscape have existed this way for ages.

The border of the property is outlined by a layered woodland that provides privacy and also creates a nestled, naturalistic setting. The horticultural palette includes a hedgerow of swamp maples (*Acer rubrum*), red cedar (*Juniperus virginiana*), American dogwood (*Cornus florida*), and various crabapples and hawthorns, underplanted by doublefile viburnum (*Viburnum plicatum tomentosum*) and dwarf burning bush (*Euonymous alatus* 'Compactus').

Dividing the front half of the property (the rolling landscape of the golf course) from the back half (formal gardens) is a grove of beeches (*Fagus*), including European (*F. sylvatica*), copper (*F. purpurea*), weeping (*F. pendula*), and fern leaf (*F. sylvatica* 'Aspleniifolia').

Hollander says that he closely collaborated with the clients on the design. He brought them to the nursery in New Jersey to see firsthand the trees he'd selected, and they were the ultimate source for the layout and character of the gardens near the house. Referring back to the Gatsby-era estates on the North Fork of Long Island, these gardens evolved along formal lines as a series of rooms.

The house, designed by architect Alan Greenberg and designer Michael Christiano, is semicircular in plan, cradling a forecourt on one side and opening to a great lawn on the other that slopes gently to the largest of the ponds on the site. The gardens work off this geometry, flanking each side of the house and leaving the lawn open, overlooking the majestic views. Beginning in the southeast quadrant of the property and working counterclockwise toward the northwest, the gardens unfold in a progression. The pool terrace is elevated eighteen inches above grade so that a relatively small (thirty-inch) fence could be used to comply with safety enclosure regulations but also preserve the views from out over the lawn. A classically themed white garden connects the pool to the main house. It is framed by a pergola draped with white-blooming wisteria (*Wisteria sinensis* 'Alba') and white dawn climbing roses. In the center, geometrical beds contain white-flowering tulips, daffodils, peonies, German and Siberian irises, Annabelle hydrangeas, Iceberg and Glamis Castle roses, lavender, catmint, hibiscus, phlox, and other perennials. As is traditional, this garden is used primarily during the nighttime, when the white appears to shimmer and reflects the moonlight.

An Italianate loggia connects this space to the terraces closest to the house and, by deriving their design from the architecture of the house itself, serve as a visual bridge to the rest of the estate. The terraces outside of the main living quarters of the house were left simple — a stone patio dropping into an expanse of grass — in order to preserve the formal majesty of the lawn. On the far side of the house the gardens pick up again with a series of garden rooms, including a fragrance garden planted with lavender, lilies, and roses; a potager or working garden where vegetables, herbs, and cut flowers are grown; a lily garden where a colored pattern of blooming has been carefully worked out beneath the shade of flowering cherry trees; to, finally, a rose garden derived from the great rose garden at the Brooklyn Botanical Garden. Hollander says he and Connelly carefully calculated the rhythmic progression of each space to create an alteration of scale and light. Some spaces are intimate, others grand. Some are bright and open, others enclosed and cradled. Linking each, however, is a close attention to detail and fine-tuning of the formal elements: architectural accents, geometrical design, and composition of plants.

Hollander terms the estate "exuberant," much like the owners, and indeed the landscape design is consciously modeled on the tradition of great estates. Like those gardens, these are meant to be strolled through on a cool summer evening while the sounds of partygoers — the chink of glasses, laughter, jazz music — float in the background. The air is fresh, frogs alight in the pond's edge, and the waft of lavender or catmint fills our nostrils.

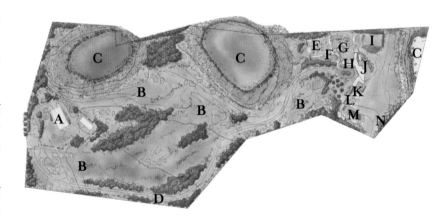

A	*Barnyard/Service Area*	H	*Potager*
B	*Golf Course*	I	*Grass Tennis Court*
C	*Ponds*	J	*House*
D	*Meandering Entry Drive*	K	*Loggia Garden*
E	*Rose Garden*	L	*White Garden*
F	*Lilac and Peony Border*	M	*Pool Area*
G	*Astrigal Garden*	N	*Butterfly Garden*

ABOVE: *The old silo was converted into a storage facility overlooking one of the multi-level greens.*

LEFT: *Bands of daylilies flank one of the potato barns incorporated into the golf course.*

ABOVE AND RIGHT: *An old storage shed was renovated as part of the golf course construction.*

FAR RIGHT: *One of the ponds which was cleaned and replanted with native shrubs and wildflowers is now home to a family of swans.*

OVERLEAF: *View across the fairways and rough to the front of the house and orangerie.*

OPPOSITE FAR LEFT: *A wrought iron gazebo planted with wisteria.*

OPPOSITE LEFT: *The loggia pergola opens onto the main terrace of the rear of the house.*

ABOVE: *A pergola draped in white wisteria surrounds the loggia terrace and white garden.*

RIGHT: *The loggia terrace of 3-by-3 foot squares of Indian sandstone with grass joints.*

OPPOSITE: *View through the white garden toward the loggia terrace.*

RIGHT: *View through the white garden to the pool area.*

BELOW RIGHT: *Steps leading up to the white garden.*

ABOVE: *The walkway to the astrigal
garden passes through the lily garden.*

ABOVE: *The astrigal garden is planted with grey-blue flowers including lavender, catmint, sea holly, globe thistle, salvia, and artemesia. The garden is punctuated with Pee Gee hydrangea trees and surrounded by a clipped yew hedge.*

LEFT: *The pool terrace is set 18 inches above grade, allowing for a 30-inch-high fence. This preserves the views out from the pool to the sweeping lawn and butterfly garden in the distance.*

BELOW LEFT: *A pool and terrace area were set off to the side of the house so as not to obstruct views from the house and white garden.*

RIGHT: *The view from the pool house pergola out across the pool and terrace.*

FAR RIGHT: *The pool house was designed by Alan Greenberg.*

BELOW: *The pool was designed without a traditional coping to give a seamless flow between water and terrace.*

LEFT: *Butterfly bushes, black-eyed Susans and daylilies in the butterfly garden.*

BELOW AND OPPOSITE: *The butterfly garden makes a transition from the formal rolling lawn off the rear of the house to the wildflower areas surrounding the pool.*

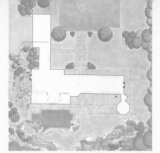

Ocean Meadow

For this beachside house designed by architect Francis Fleetwood, Ed Hollander created a transitional landscape that relates to the climate and topography found at the ocean's edge. Beginning at the entrance drive, which is planted with a single row of apple trees that refer back to the agricultural context of the area, the landscape unfolds as a low-lying, scrubby tapestry of spaces sharply delineated by microclimates. Along one side of the drive (which itself is pushed to one side of the property) is an ensemble of shrubbery raised on an earthen berm to enclose sunken basketball and tennis courts. The ensemble includes several varieties of white hydrangea — a staple of this seaside vacation area's landscape vernacular — that are resilient to the tough conditions of salt and wind. These include Annabelle, such *Hydrangea macrophylla* varieties as 'Sister Therese,' and the lacecap Lanarth white and the *H. paniculata* varieties 'tardiva' and 'unique.' The design is calculated to give a sequence of bloom from late June through September, and remind the viewer of an old-fashioned, lushly planted country lane.

AS THE HOUSE COMES INTO VIEW IT APPEARS THROUGH A LACE CURTAIN OF MATURE HONEY LOCUSTS THAT WERE CHOSEN TO CREATE A SCULPTED, "WINDSWEPT" LOOK. THE HOUSE ITSELF ACTS AS A SCREEN OR DOORWAY THROUGH WHICH THE OCEAN CAN BE GLIMPSED BEYOND. Working closer to the house, the richness of the landscape gives way to a more spartan seashore quality. Here the plants are chosen for their ability to withstand sea spray and high winds, a choice both practical and aesthetic, creating a progression that becomes increasingly harmonious with the natural dune landscape at the ocean's edge.

Unlike most oceanfront properties, where the house is placed as close to the water as possible, the architect decided that it would be smarter to pull this house back and site it farther from the water. As a result, the views from the house incorporate the dune and the scrubby vegetation, creating a more complete and richer presentation of nature.

TOP: *The entry drive is lined with white flowering hydrangea, which help to screen the tennis and basketball courts set below grade.*

ABOVE: *The entry walk, a diamond pattern of 2- by 2-foot bluestone slabs, transitions to the front lawn as pavers "slip away" into the grass.*

RIGHT: *The negative edge pool was designed to visually connect the rear terrace of the house to the ocean in the distance.*

As we move through the house, which occupies that transitional zone between land and sea, the microclimatic changes occur quickly and over a very short space. Within just a few yards there are different soil, wind, salt, and temperature conditions, which are reflected in the plant palette by the presence of windswept grasses, rugosa rose varieties, and "wild" flowering perennials that look like they could have escaped from the native dune but which were intentionally sited for effect.

Around the western side of the house, in a small space at the edge of the narrow lot, Hollander carved a small rock garden into the dune where it is protected from the winds and salt spray. This is planted with lavender and creeping winter berry and provides an excellent vantage to study the transition between the agricultural, orthogonal landscape on one side of the house and the wild, seashore dune landscape on the other.

Everything about the design of the ocean-facing side of the house refers outward to the dynamic view — from the lack of tall vegetation (which would focus attention inward) to the placement of a negative edge pool. As a result, the landscape is best read as a sequence, moving from front to back, from inward to outward, from lush farmland to rolling seashore. The landscape is also intensely useful, addressed to the needs of a multigenerational family that occupies it for frequent get-togethers. Some members may want to play tennis away from the spray and wind; others may want to go for a walk on the beach; others may stay on the terrace, sort of straddling both worlds. The total property area is small, but through the use of a cogent spatial organization Hollander was able to make it seem commodious.

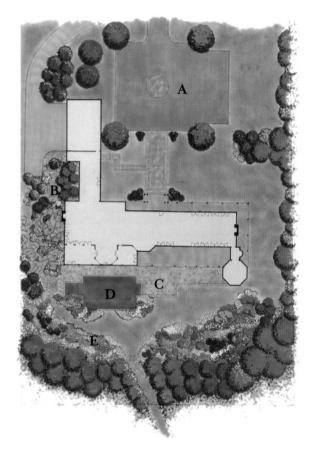

To fit all of these "programs" (as designers call client needs) into a single design required making sharp distinctions in the landscape. The clearest of these is the distinction between the old agricultural landscape on the north side of the house, which is used to site most of the active recreation spaces, and the ocean landscape on the south side, which is intended for more passive uses. Much of the design strives to heighten this already existing division. For instance, the driveway culminates in a large, square autocourt on perfect axis with the great room of the house. The formality is accented by an overly wide walkway of bluestone, patterned in rigid geometrical form, given the barest definition by lines of boxwood. On the other side, the landscape drops off into curving, informal topography before eventually dissolving into the dune. Rather than making design details like stone and plants the focus of attention, the emphasis is on the natural, stunning view.

"Great care was taken to sculpt the landscape so that it felt like it was resting upon a natural dune that was part of the existing transition zone," says Hollander's partner Maryanne Connelly. To increase the illusion, plants from the beach were brought upland as far as possible to "blend the house landscape seamlessly with the native landscape."

A *Entry Court*
B *Sunken Rock Garden*
C *Rear Terrace*
D *Negative Edge Pool*
E *Transitional Dune Garden*

RIGHT: *The sunken rock garden creates an idyllic setting for an outdoor shower.*

BELOW: *A spa is located at one end of the pool to preserve the integrity of the negative edge.*

FAR RIGHT: *Looking out over the pool to dunes and ocean beyond.*

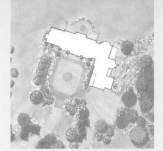

Stone Wall

O n old farmland in Fairfield County, Connecticut, stands this stone manor surrounded by gardens. The house was designed by Boris Baronovich, who used stone to create a nineteenth-century manor residence that works intelligently with the century-old walls that crisscross the woods in the area. CONNELLY AND HOLLANDER DECIDED TO MAKE A MAJESTIC SWEEP OF LAWN, WHICH CASCADES GRACEFULLY DOWN A SLOPE TO THE WOODS, THE CENTRAL FEATURE OF THE DESIGN. The house sits along a rise, thus the lawn in a way forms a plinth for the architecture, allowing it to rise in a stately manner from the landscape. Stone walls run from the base of the house out into the landscape, providing a kind of visual transition from the living space to the landscape. They also create a connection to the stone-walled horse paddocks in the area. The screen of trees delineating the boundary between properties was thinned, allowing Connelly to "borrow" views from the surrounding landscape, including the grazing thoroughbreds in the adjoining fields.

At one end of the house lies an orchard of fruiting apple and crabapple trees, which is gridded in a formal presentation. It is also a highlight for the children who, Hollander notes, like to eat the apples and toss them at the golden retrievers. At the other end of the house, the architectural walls connect with a very large, formal pool that stands as an architectural statement in its own right. Surrounding the pool is a crescent-shaped cutting garden meant to provide both an attractive complement to the fence around the pool and a separation between the lawn panel and the pool paving. "The garden at a house like this," notes Maryanne Connelly, "needs to be something that can be enjoyed every day."

ABOVE: *View through the pool gates to the pool house by Boris Baronovich.*

LEFT: *Looking over the pool fence to the meadow and equestrian track in the distance.*

RIGHT: *By setting the pool on a raised plinth above grade, a 30-inch fence is placed on top of an 18-inch-high wall opening up views from within the pool area.*

Immediately next to the kitchen is a garden walk with edible plants that can be enjoyed year-round. This gives way to a dining terrace that envelops a specimen river birch (*Betula nigra*). This terrace has a second viewing terrace overlooking the grand lawn.

The pool and pool structure are architectural statements that work in conjunction with the house and in opposition to the soft lawn. Hollander and Connelly say the challenge on this project was to recognize and accentuate the grandness of the architecture and the setting and also make the spaces livable and human. They chose to employ a kind of counterpoint, in which sharp, architectonic elements like walls and terraces are softened by drifts of plantings and majestic views. The pool provides an excellent example of this. They began with an extensive palette of hard elements, including a formal, balanced terrace and large retaining walls topped by short picket fences (carefully calibrated to meet legal requirements). By raising the pool up on these retaining walls, which allowed the use of short fences, the space was opened up to the surrounding meadow and made to seem a part of it. Below, the ground plane is organized as a display garden of summer flowering shrubs and flowers, including blue lace and Pee Gee hydrangeas, David Austin roses in shades of white, peach, and pink, and such perennials as catmint, Russian sage, phlox, Japanese iris, and Casa Blanca lilies that soften and enliven the scene. Hollander likens the technique to painting. The first step is creating the underlying structure, the lines of the objects in the painting — which in this case are the stone walls and architectural structures. The plant material is then overpainted like chiaroscuro, at once softening and highlighting the entire composition. The result is a landscape evocative of the nineteenth-century landscape painting.

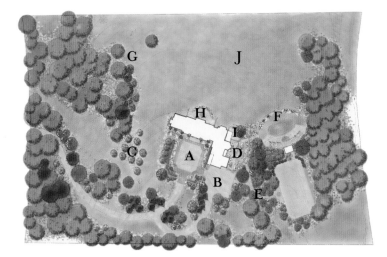

A *Entry Court*
B *Service Court*
C *Orchard*
D *Semicircular Wall Garden*
E *Birch Grove Walk*
F *Pool Area*
G *Golf green*
H *Entertaining Terrace*
I *Dining Terrace*
J *New Lawn and Meadow*

ABOVE: *View of granite entry court medal-lion to front door and loggia entry of house designed by Boris Baronovich.*

RIGHT: *Connection from service court to entry court.*

FAR RIGHT: *View to entry drive through stone columns flanked by specimen Armstrong red maples.*

ABOVE: *Walkway planted with boxwood to loggia entry.*

RIGHT: *Eden roses embrace a stone column.*

OPPOSITE: *Stepping-stone walkway to pool through a series of curved wall gardens.*

LEFT: *A fountain and spa seem to flow from the pool house terrace down to the pool itself.*

TOP: *A viewing terrace of Iowa fleck limestone provides seating areas around the pool and spa.*

ABOVE: *The oval pool is bordered by a 30-inch stone coping transitioning to lawn as one looks over the pool from the terrace below.*

Rolling Fields

For this country residence, Hollander Design wanted to recall the agricultural traditions of the region. One strong reason for this was the client's plan to establish a horse farm on the front part of the property. It is through this area — treated at present as a large field — that the magnificent entrance drive proceeds. It is set off to one side in order to allow space for the horse farm and then sweeps off, once clear of an adjacent property line, in a grand gesture reminiscent of the romantic estate drives of the nineteenth century. The entire length is lined by Red Sunset maples, a stately deciduous specimen that turns a brilliant red in fall. Beneath the lowest branches the wide expanse of the surrounding countryside comes in glimpses. The views are splendid and form the *raison d'être* of the design. In the distance the patterned rows of a working farm come into view.

The large house, designed by Francis Fleetwood, is situated at the back of the property, overlooking a quiet pond. THE VIEWS ARE SWEEPING, AND IN ORDER TO ACCENTUATE THEM AND GIVE DEPTH, HOLLANDER AND CONNELLY PLANTED A LOW-LYING MEADOW AS A TRANSITIONAL BORDER ALONG THE EDGE OF THE WATER. THIS SETS UP A VISUAL STRUCTURE OF COLOR AND LIGHTNESS, AGAINST WHICH THE DARK BLUE OF THE WATER APPEARS MORE VIBRANT.

The gardens in front of the house are arranged in radiating arcs that complement the curvature of the house. The idea here was to create a low-lying composition that was bold and powerful that spoke about the rustic nature of the local agricultural context. The gardens were lovingly planted by Denise Puccinelli into swaths of color, using a palette of such

LEFT: *View from meadow over sweeping lawn to rear of house.*

RIGHT: *A spa is set into the pool with broad shallow steps on either side. The pergola provides shade and a transition from the pool area to the garden behind.*

flowering shrubs and perennials as Lockinch butterfly bush, caryopteris, and Russian sage. The gardens are given form by two low stone walls and the spacing of crabapple trees. The fulcrum of the space, around which both the garden and house are shaped, is a circular autocourt punctuated by a flagpole. Behind the house the pool and associated terrace were placed off to the side of the main vista down to the pond. A formal garden area with low boxwood hedges and tree roses connects the screened porch and family room area to the pool. The pool itself is designed to allow for different uses by the family. Broad shallow stairs line either side of the spa leading into the pool and allow for friends and family to lounge while others can swim laps. A broad pergola of similar architectural style to the rear veranda provides shade and creates a transition area to a broad semicircular garden area contained within a white picket fence. The entire pool area is set up on a plinth to allow for views over the rose-covered fences down to the meadow and pond. A large curved stone terrace provides a room for entertaining when the doors of the living room are thrown open. The gently curving form is echoed by the roll of the lawn and the shoreline of the pond.

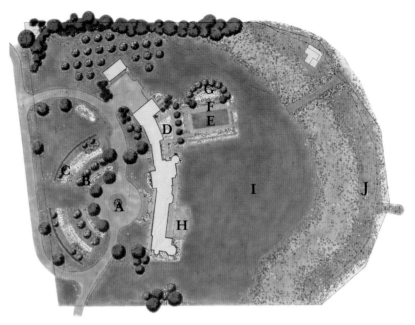

A	Entry Court	F	Pergola
B	Circular Wall at Entry Garden	G	Pool Garden
C	Circular Entry Garden	H	Entertaining Terrace
D	Formal Garden	I	Rolling Lawn
E	Pool	J	Meadow

ABOVE: *Curved stone walls form a
backdrop for masses of Sea Foam roses.*

ABOVE: *Behind the walls. flowering crabapple trees reinforce the circular forms as do beds of Russian sage, salvia, and Hydrangea tardiva.*

LEFT: *View over the entertaining terrace to the pool area.*

TOP: *A formal garden of low boxwood hedges and bedding plants provides a view from the screened porch.*

ABOVE: *The garden beds frame a walkway to the house.*

OPPOSITE: *View from the shade of the pool pergola to the screened porch and rear of the house.*

ABOVE: *The spa is built into the shallow end of the pool with broad shallow steps on either side allowing for lounging and lap swimming.*

RIGHT: *Flowers in the pergola garden behind the pool.*

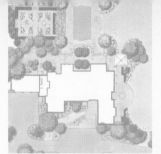

Hidden Paths

ocated in leafy woodlands, this five-acre summer place has been a ten-year ongoing experiment for Hollander Design. "Every season we do a new project on a new piece of land," Ed Hollander says. As a result, the property has become for the firm a kind of landscape laboratory. Here the firm has had the opportunity to perfect certain design ideas that may be more nascent or emerging in other projects.

The home was designed by New York architect Boris Baronovich. The main theme of the landscape is *connection*. Years of work have been spent trying to get the landscape spaces of the garden to interrelate with the architectural spaces of the house. "All of my clients are interested in plants, which is great," he says. "But I always tell them, 'Before you even think of plants, let's get the spaces right.'"

THE GARDENS ARE LAID OUT AROUND THE HOUSE IN OUT-WARDLY EVOLVING LAYERS THAT PROGRESS FROM FORMAL AND INTIMATE TO GRADUALLY MORE INFORMAL AND OPEN. Hollander says he was trying to create a sense of softness in the landscape that both extends such architectural elements as the small, intimate terraces and creates contrast to the high gables and angular roofline of the house. But the native landscape dictated much of the design. The overgrown woods that characterize this area and provide the surrounding landscape context were edited and shaped to create a mosaic of green spaces tailored to individual uses. The natural sloping of the land — the remnants of dunes that once existed here — suggested the overall pattern of the landscape, which opens and closes serially between sunny lawns and areas of dense plantings, or between recreational areas and enclosed gardens.

Arriving at the entry to the property, one is greeted by a cut in the dunes that at once invites the viewer into the property and creates a sense of mystery and anticipation. The road is planted with a formal row of native swamp maples (*Acer rubrum*) that are adapted to the wet clay soils on this part of the property. Their vivid autumn foliage — a deep russet red — provides a foil to the more natural plantings beyond which we find a dense layering that is used to create a sense of privacy along the drive and to form green walls that separate the landscape into distinct rooms and enclose each garden. The key to the design is the transitional moment

ABOVE: *A dark blue pool sits in quiet reflection surrounded by a terrace of Arizona sandstone.*

RIGHT: *Looking from pool lawn over an informal bed with Graham Thomas and Heritage English roses to the lower lawn and pool fence in the distance.*

between each of these gardens where subtle changes in light and shade (effected by careful screening of shade trees) heighten the sense of moving from one place to another.

A careful manipulation of the ground plane is used to demarcate divisions in the garden. Following the main transverse axis, which runs in an east-west direction from the main entry hall across the width of the property, we come first to a small sitting area structured by four plane trees planted on an orthogonal grid. Just beyond lies the pool. It is actually quite close, but raised on a plinth of creamy, beige sandstone that makes it seem visually individuated. The architectural framing is a dry-set Pennsylvania fieldstone retaining wall complemented by an arc of yellowwood trees (*Cladrastis lutea*) underplanted by shade-tolerant oakleaf hydrangea (*Hydrangea quercifolia*) and Dixie Wood ferns. A pergola draped with wisteria and roses — a gesture meant to invoke the great Country Place estates of the early twentieth century — runs along the length of the pool and creates a destination within this space. It also sets up a secondary transecting axis, thus drawing the eye and the mind further into the property, and enfolding yet more spatial and relational complexity. Amazingly, the property comprises a mere five acres: At times it feels like fifty. The landscape material evokes a horticultural wonderland. Beyond the pool lies a fragrance garden composed with viburnum, daphne, sweet bay magnolia, summersweet, and lily of the valley. The forest surrounding the property and enclosing each garden is layered with stewartia, saucer and star magnolias, flowering dogwoods, Carolina silverbells, and Nellie Stevens, American, and inkberry hollies. These are set against an edited "canvas" of native yellowwood, swamp maple, sweet gum, and oak that are underplanted by thickets of viburnums, laurels, leucothoes, drifts of daffodils, bleeding hearts, and ferns. This dense, multitextured screen provides an evolving scene through the seasons. Shrub borders closer to the house are composed of paniculata hydrangeas, butterfly bush, David Austin roses, and white-blooming Annabelle and Lanarth hydrangeas that create waves and blocks of artful color in the summer months.

Perhaps the greatest connection between architecture and landscape occurs off the dining pavilion at the corner of the house, where informal and formal spaces interconnect. Here the landscape serves as a stitching element between these, making a visual transition through the interplay of such architectural elements as stairs, walls, and columns. A small passageway leads the eye away from the house and out to a gently sloping lawn, which is meant to remind the viewer of the vernacular landscape, but which also provides a large sunny space that contrasts with the enclosed space of the dining terrace. The main axis of the house extends into this lawn and culminates in a semicircle of pink flowering crabapples and perennials layered to create a perceptible curve in the landscape. A path magically appears adjacent to this border where one almost disappears under a mound of white-flowering tardiva and Pee Gee hydrangeas. It leads eventually to the guest house and the cutting garden, the latter an intimate space enclosed within a low, natural cedar picket fence and a rose-covered arbor, planted and cared for by master gardener Carol Mercer.

Hollander says that the key to designing places like this is to create a sense of elegance and age without being too pat and boring. Everything is balanced. A traditional detail — a classical allée of arborvitae, for instance — needs to be softened by a lacy, layered wall of woodland shrubs. Together they create a dialogue.

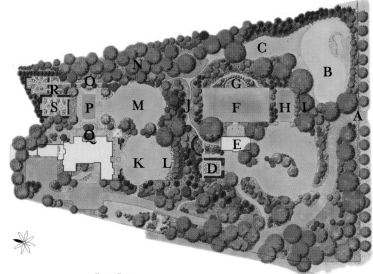

A *Entry Drive*
B *Golf Area*
C *Children's Garden*
D *Cutting Garden*
E *Guest House*
F *Tennis Court*
G *Tennis Viewing Terrace*
H *Basketball Court*
I *Dune Top Seating Area*
J *The White Walk*

K *Formal Lawn*
L *Semicircular Border*
M *Pool Lawn*
N *Fragrance Lawn*
O *Fountain*
P *Pool Area*
Q *Sycamore Bosque Dining Terrace*
R *Potager*
S *White Garden*

OPPOSITE: *The dining terrace is set at the same elevation as the kitchen and covered porch to allow easy access for outdoor meals.*

ABOVE: *Broad steps pierce a fieldstone wall to sweep up to the pool.*

RIGHT: *A shaded pavilion draped in blue lace and Annabelle hydrangea is another location for a peaceful meal.*

OPPOSITE: *Four sycamore trees frame the view of the pool area while providing shade for the dining terrace.*

ABOVE: *The pool terrace, paved with Arizona sandstone to stay cool in the summer is shaded by a wisteria- and rose-covered pergola.*

RIGHT: *The upper terrace has a low wall with water cascading from cut stone into a pool below.*

OPPOSITE: *View from the potager through the white garden down to the house. Four Leyland cypress trees serve as anchors.*

ABOVE: *The white garden lovingly cared for by Carol Mercer has boxwood edges and a lattice pavilion with two benches tucked away inside.*

FOLLOWING PAGES: *Hidden paths.*

BELOW: *A natural cedar picket gate and arbor, flanked by English hollies marks the entry to the garden.*

TOP: *The path to the guest house pokes through the fence inviting one to visit.*

ABOVE: *The geometry of square pavers with grass joints is softened by lush layers of white and blue lacecap hydrangeas.*

OVERLEAF: *View from the informal dune terrace to the golf green tucked away in one corner of the property.*

View over the golf green.

Landscape Elements

Walls and Stairs

Walls and stairs are two of the most commonly used built elements in any landscape design. They are most frequently utilized to create spaces. They can simultaneously divide areas while also connecting similar or disparate rooms in the landscape. Changing levels with as few as three stairs changes one's perspective of both the upper and lower spaces. The change of pace caused by walking up or down stairs causes one to slow and also aids in the feeling of progressing from one room to another. Stairs can provide the transition from a more formal, built landscape to a less formal area.

Frequently walls are built to aid in the transition of levels within a property. When one is confronted with a piece of property where many activities will occur and there is a significant amount of topography, walls become essential elements in the landscape.

Walls also allow us to draw the architecture of the building out into the landscape. By utilizing the same or similar types of stone as the building, the landscape walls can serve to create outdoor rooms in a manner similar to that of the house. This also helps to create an ambiguous line between the indoor and outdoor spaces.

(1) *Slabs of fieldstone serve as both treads and risers.* (2) *Informal stone slabs.* (3) *Stone risers with a sloping grass walk.* (4) *Cut granite walls.* (5) *A curving stone wall creates a backdrop for a garden bed while transitioning to the landscape beyond.* (6) *Fieldstone treads and risers.* (7) *Granite slabs create steps up to the pool area.* (8) *Cut fieldstone treads and risers connect the walls on either side.* (9) *Informal, narrow, curving stairs.* (10) *Formal curved stairs of Indian sandstone treads and Westchester granite risers.* (11) *Stone stairs.* (12) *Curving stone stairs and walls.* (13) *Formal stone garden walls flow up the stairs.* (14) *A picket fence sits on top of a low stone wall with columns to punctuate an opening.* (15) *Sandstone paving and wall copings with Pennsylvania fieldstone walls.* (16) *Pennsylvania fieldstone walls with a lesss formal "Dutch" coping.*

Terraces and Seating Areas

Terraces and seating areas are spaces where people live, eat, and recreate in the landscape. A seating area can be as informal as two Adirondack chairs sitting on a few slabs of natural stone. It can also be as grand and formal as is needed to accommodate the functions which will occur there. Frequently we will design a smaller, more intimate dining terrace and also a larger terrace off the living room for grander functions. The connection between indoor and outdoor rooms is very critical where outdoor terraces are immediately adjacent to similar interior living spaces. Scale, proportion, and material all need to be considered in the design of these terrace spaces. In many cases these areas are surrounded by low seating walls and have stairs that connect them to other areas. All of these structures need to be thought of as elements of a larger composition.

144

(1) Sandstone with white creeping thyme joints. (2) Bluestone terrace transitions to slabs with grass joints. (3) Fieldstone wall borders a stone dining terrace. (4) Misty rose terrace and coping on wall. (5) Canvas awning shades a living terrace. (6) Dining terrace set in a fragrant herb garden. (7) Wisteria-covered pavilion shades a seating area. (8) Random rectangular bluestone terrace. (9) Wooden deck leads down to dock at the side of the bay. (10) Beach house mahogany deck transitions into dune-side plantings.

Fences and Gates

(1) *Picket fence with gate.* (2) *Split rail fence with Eden roses bordering drive.* (3) *Rough-sawn oak paddock fence covered in climbing roses.* (4) *Unstained cedar picket fence and arbor around a cutting garden.* (5) *Curved cedar twig fencing creates a rustic feeling.* (6) *A curved gate announces the entry to the garden.* (7) *A fence patterned after a Charles Rennie Mackintosh design separates a dining area from the street beyond.* (8) *A curved fence leads to a gate at the top of the stairs.* (9) *A flat-topped gate breaks a fence line draped in clematis.* (10) *A 24-inch-high fence on top of a 24-inch-high wall complies with pool enclosure codes while allowing views out of the pool area.* (11) *A concave picket gate within a fence line forms an entry to the pool.* (12) *An entry gate for a formal property.* (13) *A translucent wrought iron gate shows off the garden path beyond.* (14) *A paddock fence lines the driveway to this farm property.* (15) *A panel gate within a stone wall.*

Fences can define and divide rooms in the landscape. They can also serve as a backdrop for a garden and provide support for vines and climbing roses. Materials can vary from wooden picket to split rail to wrought iron. The material and design of the fence should complement the other architectural elements in the landscape. Gates are the doorways that provide the transition from one area to the next. They can be identical to the surrounding fence or totally different. Varying the design of a fence with a concave or convex curve calls out the location, with the implication that a path lies beyond.

Arbors and Pergolas

Arbors and pergolas are architectural structures that can be rooms unto themselves or accents within a larger composition. Pergolas provide shade and a roof for a garden room. An arbor creates a transitionary space that is a node in the circulation throughout a landscape. Their formality and materials can vary to be appropriate within the context of the larger vernacular landscape and a more direct extension of the building architecture into the landscape. A pergola usually has a minimum of six columns supporting a series of wooden members or lattice. An arbor usually has two to four smaller posts that support a curving or flat open roof structure. Arbors frequently contain gates that serve to separate and connect the pathways in a garden.

(1) A poolside pergola creates a shaded seating area covered in honeysuckle and clematis. (2) A lattice room is created under the pergola. (3) A pergola that is an architectural extension of the house into the landscape. (4) An elegant, round-columned pergola set into a poolside garden. (5) Wrought iron hoops create a wisteria-lined walkway leading to the pool. (6) A long pergola covers a walkway leading to the pool. (7) A pergola creates a garden room when bathed in old-fashioned rambling roses. (8) A Nantucket picket fence and arbor cloaked in climbing roses. (9) An arbor buried in Sweet Autumn clematis forms a gateway to the pool area. (10) A grand pergola creates a connection between house, tennis court, and pool areas. (11) A rustic cedar arbor identifies a gateway. (12) A pergola with lattice walls creates a shaded seating area with views out to the rose garden.

Pools, Spas, and Fountains

Water serves many purposes within a landscape. From a functional point of view pools and spas represent an idealized form of summer recreation. They are major built elements within a landscape and need to be considered at the earliest stage of site master planning. The design of any pool or spa is tied to use, the formality and scale of the property, and other materials found in the landscape. Because of the essential role water plays in human life, pools and spas are never purely decorative elements. Reflecting pools and fountains can add both serenity and drama to a landscape. Both the sight and sound of water need to be considered in any design.

(1) *A pool with built-in spa and broad shallow stairs allows lap swimming, lounging, and spa enjoyment.* (2) *A deep blue pool reflects the architectural and natural elements in the adjacent area.* (3) *Late afternoon sun illuminates the stone wall supporting a negative edge.* (4) *A negative or infinity edge allows the pool to form a waterfall backdrop for the seating area.* (5) *A reflecting pool as a landscape focal point.* (6) *A bubbling fountain feeds a cascading rill leading down to a more dramatic fountain.* (7) *A 20- by 60-foot pool with half-moon spa at the shallow end.* (8) *A circular spa "overflows" into the naturalized pool below.* (9) *Pool and spa set within a terra-cotta terrace.* (10) *Pool stairs can be places to sit and relax.* (11) *A stepping-stone within a rill.* (12) *Sheer descent waterfalls.* (13) *Broad stairs along the entire shallow end of a pool.*

14

15

16

17

(14) *A stone wall creates a negative edge to the pool in summer and is one of a series of walls on the property in the winter months.* (15) *Brick terrace around a "Caribbean blue" pool.* (16) *Water flows from a shallow children's pool down stairs and a rill to the main pool.* (17) *A "no wave" lap pool allows water to flow over a negative edge and through a cut stone trough bordering the terrace.* (18) *A half-moon spa set on the side of the pool.* (19) *A spa balances the entry stairs in the pool.*

18

19

Orchards, Meadows, and Ponds

(1) *A boathouse allows access into a newly constructed pond.* (2) *Fruiting pear trees line a country drive with peach and apple orchards beyond the fence.* (3) *Flowering crabapples in an orchard pattern surround a drive.* (4) *Wildflowers transition to lawn areas adjacent to the house.* (5) *Apple trees create a border to a property.* (6,7,8,9) *Wildflower meadows.*

Incorporating more natural landscape elements such as meadows and ponds into a property can reduce maintenance costs while enhancing wildlife value. Wildflower meadows can form transitions between planted areas and more natural surroundings while providing stunning seasonal beauty. Species selection for each meadow can be formulated to work as a part of the larger ecosystem. Orchards provide an appropriate context in post agricultural landscapes while providing blossoms in the spring and fruit in the fall.

Recreational Elements

Recreational facilities are components of many landscapes. Basketball and tennis courts are large elements that are usually regulated by local zoning codes. Their placement needs to be considered early in the site design process. Sinking the courts and surrounding them with walls, lattice fencing, or dense, layered plantings are all techniques used to minimize the visual impact of these structures. Golf greens need full sun and good air circulation. The best greens are part of a complex with sand traps and bunkers that allow for a variety of play.

(1) *A golf green and bunker complex.*
(2) *Tennis court with natural cedar posts and netting as fence.* (3) *A tennis court sunken into the landscape.* (4) *A deco-turf tennis court surrounded with borders of hydrangea, viburnum, and holly.*
(5) *Lattice fencing with Sweet Autumn clematis vines.* (6) *Tennis seating terrace set within hydrangea beds.* (7) *A putting green and tees allow for practice and fun.*
(8) *Details of fence post, netting, and drainage trench.* (9) *Half-court basketball.*

Walkways and Paths

All of the elements within and between garden areas are connected by paths and walkways. The material and design of these elements help to give definition to the space while also creating the feel of the space. They can be formal or informal, straight or curved, narrow or wide or varying in width. They can be made of stone, brick, or other masonry materials. They can be made of gravel, wood, or even grass. Paths can be constructed of natural or cut stone with plants or grass growing between the stones. It is critical to pick a material, layout, and design for the walk that speaks to the overall character of the space it moves within and connects to. Paths and walkways are essential components of any landscape and essential in creating transitions from one space to the next.

(1) *Old brick laid in a herringbone pattern.* (2) *Stone slabs step in a Zen-like pattern through the Japanese garden.* (3) *A simple gravel walkway.* (4) *A natural fieldstone garden walkway.* (5) *A fieldstone path set amongst shrub roses and creeping thyme.* (6) *Mosaic bluestone with grass joints.* (7) *Bluestone squares with grass joints.* (8) *Curving gravel garden walks with wooden edging.* (9) *Walkways can widen at certain points.* (10) *A grass path through a garden.* (11) *Wooden boardwalks.* (12) *Gravel beach path.* (13) *Bluestone entry walk with creeeping thyme joints.*

Acknowledgments

A heartfelt thank-you to all of the dedicated, enthusiastic and, talented members of the office team over the past ten years. This includes the present staff of Will Harris, Roger Zhang, Steven Cantor, Rick Williams, Howard Williams, Jeannine Freed, Jennifer Horn, Jorge Leal, Nai-wei Hsiung, and Stone Shen.

To all of our clients — we could not have accomplished this without their trust and confidence which allowed our vision to grow with their families.

To those dedicated people who have done the hard work to bring our vision to fruition: Whitmores, Lewis and Valentine, J&R Landscaping, Hrens, Marders, Frankenbachs Deerfield, Alfredos, Ceci Brothers, and Tarva DiRoma; the masons at 7 Sons, Mike Cobuzzi, Paul Schneider, and Chris Ryan have always added their craftsmanship to our designs; master pool and waterfall builders John Tortorella, Imperial Gunite, Ed Guillo, Wagner, Shoreline, Peppinger and Cipriano who have made the aquatic parts of our landscapes so successful; thanks to all of the men on bulldozers who sculpt the land — Frank Berry, Danny Shields, Carmine DiSunno, Ken Helstowski, Rob Alfredo, and Ricciardi Brothers; to Bruce Peterson and his irrigation specialists who, no matter how unreasonable the request, can still get the jobs done with a smile; to all the people who maintain these properties: Tim Blenk, Ron Jawin, Sean Dunne, Harlan Foley, Mike Tuths, Carol Mercer, and Julie Reisdorff. And of course to the one and only Fano.

To Rich Warren and Larry Liebman who work tirelessly behind the scenes getting the permits for this work.

To Emma Hill, our first client, and Phillip Tomlinson, whose editing and writing made a difference.

To David Narbett for the illustrative plans.

A special thank-you to the architects with whom we have had the honor to collaborate on these many projects including: Boris Baranovich, Barnes Coy, Deborah Berke, Peter Cook, Cooper Robertson, Ferguson Shamamian, Mark Finlay, Harry Fischman, Francis Fleetwood, Alex Gorlin, Ira Grandberg, Alan Greenberg, Frank Greenwald, Steven Holl, John Laffey, Leroy Street Architects, MCM Architects, Mark Mathews, Ken Nadler, Bruce Nagel, Pam Pospisil, Claus Rademacher, Lawrence Randolph, Rebecca Rasmussen, Kevin Roche, John David Rose, Gary Savitsky, Sears and Sears, Shope Reno Wharton, Skolnick Design Partnership, Fred Stelle, Robert A. M. Stern, Mojo Stumer, James Thompson, Charles Young, Zwirko & Ortmann.

To John Collins, Tom Schraudenbach, and the people at The Delta Group who encouraged us to dedicate our heart and soul to each project.

And finally to Mercury, the guardian of the gate and the lunch room.

Photography Credits

BETSY PINOVER SCHIFF
Front Cover, 2-3, 24T, 24M, 24B, 24-25, 28T, 28B, 28-29, 31T, 31B, 33, 34-35, 40T, 40B, 41TL, 41TR, 41B, 42T, 42B, 44B, 45TR, 45BR, 48, 48-49, 52, 53TL, 53TR, 53B, 54, 54TL, 54TR, 54BL, 54BR, 56, 57, 58T, 58B, 59, 60L, 60TR, 60MR, 64T, 64B, 65, 68, 69T, 69BL, 69BR, 70T, 75BL, 75BR, 76, 77T, 77B, 78, 79T, 79B, 98T, 98B, 98-99, 102T, 102B, 102-103, 128, 129T, 130, 131T, 131B, 134TR, 134MR, 134BR, 136-137, 137TR, 137MR, 137BL, 138-139, 143 (#15), 145 (#4, 5), 147 (#2, 4, 9, 12, 13), 149 (#3, 9, 10), 151 (#7, 9), 153 (#19), 155 (#2, 3, 5, 9), 156, 157 (#4, 9), 159 (#10, 12)

CHARLES MAYER
Back Cover, 1, 12TR, 12BL, 12BR, 12-13, 16TL, 16BL, 16R, 17, 18T, 18B, 19, 20-21, 21R, 22-23, 23R, 32L, 45L, 60BR, 61T, 61B, 62R, 62-63, 84T, 84BL, 84BR, 85T, 85B, 88L, 88R, 89T, 89B, 90, 91T, 91B, 104T, 104B, 104-105, 108T, 108BL, 108BR, 109T, 109B, 110TL, 110TR, 110B, 111, 112-113, 113T, 113B, 114, 114-115, 120-121, 121B, 129B, 132, 133, 134L, 135, 141 (Terraces and Seating Areas Detail, Pools, Spas and Fountains Detail, Recreational Elements Detail, Walkways and Paths Detail), 142, 143 (#4, 5, 6, 8, 9, 10, 11, 12), 144, 145 (#6, 7, 8, 9, 10), 147 (#5, 8, 14), 148, 149 (#4, 6, 7, 8, 11), 150T, 150B, 151 (#3, 4, 5, 6, 10, 11, 12, 13), 152 (#14, 16), 153 (#17), 155 (#4), 157 (#2, 5, 6, 7, 8), 158, 159 (#4, 5, 6, 7, 9, 11)

TORI BUTT
30-31, 32TR, 32BR, 36, 36-37, 43, 44T, 46-47, 47T, 47M, 47B, 70B, 70-71, 74-75, 80, 80-81, 86-87, 92, 93, 94T, 94B, 95TL, 95TR, 95B, 96T, 96B, 97, 118, 119, 121T, 122, 123T, 123B, 141 (Fences and Gates Detail, Arbors and Pergolas Detail), 145 (#3), 146, 147 (#6, 10), 149 (#12), 152 (#15), 157 (#3)

DENCY KANE
141 (Walls and Stairs Detail), 143 (#13, 14)

STEVE TURNER
14-15, 26, 26-27, 38, 39, 51, 66-67, 72-73, 82, 83, 100, 101, 107, 116, 117, 127

ED HOLLANDER
124, 124-125, 143 (#2, 3, 16), 145 (#2), 147 (#3, 7, 11), 149 (#5), 153 (#18), 155 (#6, 7, 8), 159 (#3, 8, 13)

MARYANNE CONNELLY
143 (#7), 147 (#15), 149 (#2), 151 (#8), 159 (#2)

CAMERA 1
Back Flap

Illustration Credit

DAVID NARBETT
12, 14, 24, 26, 36, 38, 48, 50, 64, 66, 70, 72, 80, 82, 98, 100, 104, 106, 114, 116, 124, 126

T	= TOP
B	= BOTTOM
M	= MIDDLE
TR	= TOP RIGHT
MR	= MIDDLE RIGHT
BR	= BOTTOM RIGHT
TL	= TOP LEFT
TM	= MIDDLE LEFT
BL	= BOTTOM LEFT